THE GOSPEL
CANNOT BE CHAINED

SEARCHING FOR GRACE
IN PAUL'S PRISON LETTERS

Mick Mooney

LIGHT
VIEW
MEDIA

Published by Lightview Media
For more information visit:
http://lightviewmedia.com

THE GOSPEL CANNOT BE CHAINED

For Paul,
Thanks

Paul's Prison Letters

FOREWORD

This book is a collection of Paul's prison letters that he wrote during his imprisonment in Rome, paraphrased, with a great deal of respect, in a way that highlights what I believe to be the heart of his message. I find it amazing that even in prison Paul still knew he was free; he still knew of a far greater reality that was his in Christ. The beauty of his message of God's love and grace in his prison letters touches my heart every time I read them. This book is an expression of my understanding of Paul's letters. I hope it blesses your heart also.

Paul's letters reveal so much of his heart of love, his joy in God's grace, and his uncompromising faith in the redemptive work of Jesus. Paul has, in a spiritual way, become one of my dearest friends; a wonderful brother in my own faith walk who has always encouraged me through his letters that I can truly live by the Spirit of God. Although

I haven't yet met him personally, I certainly appreciate the letters he wrote to me, to you, and to all who are part of the body of Christ.

I didn't approach paraphrasing Paul's letters with the mindset that I was rewriting Scripture, but rather, respectfully attempting to clarify the heart of a dear friend who is no longer with us. The best way to read this book is in rest. Relax, and read it as if you are reading a few letters from a dear brother in Christ who is writing you a personal letter to remind you of the wonderful reality of God's grace.

As this is not a Bible, but rather a modern expression of four letters from a friend, I have not formatted it in the way modern Bibles format Paul's letters. There are no verses or chapters. The best way to read these letters is in one sitting, as you would with any letter you received from a friend today.

I hope that through reading my interpretation of Paul's letters it helps highlight for you his message of love and grace in whatever Bible translation you normally read.

Blue skies,
Mick Mooney

THE GOSPEL
CANNOT BE CHAINED

4

EPHESIANS

6

EPHESIANS

Paul, a man transformed by grace, born again in love and set apart, according to God's plan, to proclaim the divine message of new life for all. To my faith-filled brothers and sisters in Ephesus: grace and peace to you, given freely to us all by our beloved Father in heaven.

How wonderful our God is; how amazing his grace! Indeed, our hearts can't help but praise him. God, the Father of our Lord Jesus, has truly blessed us beyond measure. For a man can earn money in order to buy things of luxury, but he cannot earn the peace of God; and what no man can earn, God has freely given us. What man could ever earn the joy of God? What man could ever earn the rest of God? No man can earn these heavenly blessings, and yet, through our faith in Jesus, God has freely given us all of them as a gift.

Oh, how he loves us. Just as the cross was planned by God before the creation of the world, so was his decision to reveal the depths of his love to all who would accept his Son. It does our hearts good to remember that God's plan has its foundations in eternity and the good news of his grace was a message stirring in his heart before time was even created. Oh, how amazing our God is! Before he began creating the universe he had already finished planning our eternal salvation; a way that all of us could be made holy, dearly loved and without blame in his sight - a gift that lasts forever. Brothers and sisters, we have good reason to rejoice, for through Jesus we have been made 'new' in God's eyes. We will never again be seen in our faults, but rather, forever seen in his grace. For, according to natural law, we were all born once through the body of our earthly mothers, but now, through divine grace, we have been born again through the body of our Lord Jesus Christ, not as children of men, but as children of God. Hallelujah.

This abundant provision of grace has not been given to us without cost, on the contrary, it cost the Son of God his life. Jesus paid the full price for every blessing upon the cross, and that is why we now freely receive all the benefits that God gives to his children. From God's perspective, all his blessings belong to us, because Jesus paid for all of them on our behalf. Jesus earned all the blessings, and then, as a perfect picture of his love for us, desired that the payment for his work would be credited to our account. How deep is his love for us that he would do such a thing? We receive everything, because we are now living in the one who paid for everything; not by our works, but by the working of his grace. We are forgiven of sins, redeemed from brokenness, and established in his love through the blood of Jesus, spilt upon the cross for us. My fellow brothers and sisters, how great is Christ's love for us? He did not withhold anything, but gave himself up freely, so that God could pour his grace upon all of us without restriction. This is not an act God does hastily; rather, he gives us an abundance of his grace with all divine wisdom and understanding. Worldly wisdom demands works, but God's wisdom offers grace – it isn't a risk to God; it is the power of God!

It now gives God great pleasure to make known to us the mystery of his will, his eternal purpose that has been stirring in his heart from the beginning: *that we can rest in his Son*. What a revelation! God doesn't want to give mankind a burden to carry, but a place to rest. This is not merely a theoretical statement; it is an ever expanding revelation. Indeed, we, as the firstfruits, have already entered into this rest, and, in the fulfillment of the ages, all things in heaven and on earth will also be made new and enter into his rest, making all things one in perfect unity under his loving care.

My dear friends, we can be certain that God doesn't give his rest to people based on their own accomplishments; on the contrary, we receive his rest through the perfect accomplishments of Christ. And now, through God's grace, we have been adopted by God himself; we have become his children and his treasured possession, not based on our flawed merits, but rather on the perfect, finished work of Christ. God planned it all before time began, and through faith in Jesus we have entered into the 'light' of that plan. God, who is now outworking everything according to the purpose of his will, has created a way so that we, who are the first to hope in Christ, can truly rest in him, know him, and boast in his love, to the praise of his glory.

How, I ask you, did we find ourselves in Christ, the one whom we find rest for our souls, salvation for our spirits and God's blessings in this life? Was it by our own efforts? Not at all! Rather, we were included in him when we heard the word of truth, the good news that through his life, sacrifice, death and resurrection we can now be included in his resurrected life. Now that you believe, you can be assured that your life is marked as a child of God with the heavenly seal, the promised Holy Spirit, given to you, to comfort you, empower you, and remind you daily of this wonderful reality. Indeed, the day is coming when we will inherit the kingdom of heaven itself. We're not only going to heaven one day as servants; we will enter triumphantly, as sons and daughters. We won't simply be part of the kingdom of heaven; rather, together with Christ, we will own it! We now belong to God, and for that reason we will inherit all that is God's, and all this is by his will - Oh, how he loves us.

It is for this very reason that I write to you, to remind both you and I of the good news of Jesus. I want you to know how Christ has filled me with joy through the news of your new found faith in him and the love you now have for one other. Indeed, since I heard of your faith, I have not stopped thanking God. I'm telling you the truth. I am so blessed to know that you too have believed upon Christ and I joyfully welcome you into his family. I can testify, with great certainty, that you have been drawn wonderfully close to him. Indeed, in Christ not one of us is kept distant. Oh, may the eyes of your heart see this beautiful reality, for it is your born-again birthright in Christ Jesus. And, just as I thank God for you all, I also pray that God would bless you beyond measure with the Spirit of wisdom and revelation, in order that you may know him more intimately, for that is his desire. Yes, I pray that you may truly understand the depths of his love; for the foundation of our faith is firmly established in his unending love.

In love, God has given us his Holy Spirit, and

that certainly is good news. His Spirit does not produce fear, hatred and bondage; on the contrary, it produces life, love and liberty. His Spirit created the universe. His Spirit raised Christ from the dead. His Spirit is powerful - wonderfully powerful! Gloriously powerful! It is this very same Spirit that is now living in you, and, through his grace, it is now at work in you.

My brothers and sisters in the Lord, stop and think about it: the very same power that was strong enough to raise Jesus from the dead, placing him at the Father's right hand in the heavens, is now dwelling in you. It is by this power that Jesus now reigns in glory. Nothing can compare to the power, authority, and dominion that Jesus now has. He is above every title that can be given; from eternity to eternity he reigns supreme - and we are in him. We have been united together as his body. And now, through our faith in him, God, in his wisdom, is bringing to fulfillment his glorious plan of mankind's redemption.

Tell me, how does it feel to know the truth? To know that you are a brand new person, cleansed and made pure in every way in the eyes of your heavenly Father? It feels glorious, I know, for I experience this same wonderful reality. How different a life we now have. For in the past we walked in the ways of darkness, lost in the foolish things this world offers, and spending all we had to buy what only broke our hearts or burdened us with guilt and shame. All of us lived in this way at one time, and, to our thinking, it was all we could hope for; gratifying the cravings of our self-absorbed ego while following its desires and thoughts. We were no different from anyone, and, based on our own merits and deeds, deserved nothing good from God. But praise God that he does not give to us based on what we deserve, but rather, he gives to us based on the reality of his graceful and loving nature, expressed through what his Son has done on our behalf. It is because of his great love for us, despite our past misdeeds, that he has given us a new life; for the riches of his mercy are truly endless. Yes, it is by his grace, and only by his grace, that we could ever receive such a blessing.

I praise God that our 'bad works' didn't disqualify us, and our 'good works' didn't qualify us. His love towards us is not at all based on our past performance, whether good or bad, but rather, his divine acceptance of us is based on the finished work of his Son upon the cross. And now, having put our faith in Jesus, we have received a covenant relationship of grace: an intimate relationship with him based on his perfect love and faithfulness to us. We can rest and rejoice in the knowledge that it is not by our works we are saved, but rather, it is because God has a nature of grace.

We are now free in his love, alive in his life, and perfectly cleansed through his forgiveness. My dear friends, as glorious as our forgiveness is, it is only a tiny fraction of what we have received. Indeed, we should rejoice that we have been given so much more. For we have been raised with Christ and seated with him in the glorious kingdom of God. I'm not suggesting this will happen one day - I'm testifying that it has already happened! When we accepted Jesus, his Spirit came to live in us, and our Spirit went to sit with him. We are now one with Jesus; both he with us as here on earth, and we with him in the heavens. What, one might ask, is God doing as we sit with him in the heavens? My siblings in Christ, he is looking at us with love and affection. He is enjoying our company and reminding us of how he sees us: holy, blameless and forever loved. He does this to reveal to our hearts, indeed, to all of creation, the incomparable riches of his grace. For the rest of eternity we will be the living proof of God's unending kindness; we are his beloved forever. Our salvation is an act of pure grace. Our adoption, new life, and redemption have nothing to do with our own efforts and everything to do with the King of kings, the One and only, Jesus our Lord. Just as Jesus was a gift to the world, so too is the salvation that we have received through him. In light of this glorious truth it's easy to understand why our boast is not in our limited ability, but in his unlimited love for us.

Therefore, remember his grace always, and remember the whole story of God's redemption plan. Remember that God first set apart the nation of Israel. He gave them the Holy Scriptures and a temporary covenant of law through which he prophesied the coming of the saviour of all mankind : Jesus Christ. It is through Jesus that this old covenant was fulfilled and the new eternal covenant has been established. It is this new covenant of grace that you have been saved into. At one time you were separated from God, but, because God is faithful, all of you who were far from God have found yourself now living in his very presence through the grace of Christ.

Previously, there was only one way, and that way was for the Jewish people. The law of their covenant excluded other nations and cultures from participating in a covenant relationship with the living God. Yet now we see how truly merciful God is, that he allowed Jesus, who is the Christ of the Jewish law, to come and fulfill all the righteous requirements of that law, bringing that covenant to fulfillment through his perfect life, ending the era of religious obligations and regulations, and establishing the promised new covenant; not according to man's nature of law, but according to God's divine nature of grace. The old, temporary covenant was exclusive to one nation, but the new, eternal covenant is available to every nation and tribe on earth. For Jesus himself has become our peace and he has made a way for all of mankind to belong to God; both those close and those far away. He died upon the cross for all people, regardless of their religious or cultural backgrounds, in order that they may come to know him and realise the profound reality that, through the sacrifice of Jesus, all mankind have been granted access to the Father through the Spirit of divine love.

Now, through the finished work of Jesus, we can all rest in confidence with the knowledge that we are citizens of heaven and members together of one household. This household is built upon the foundation of the gospel message that I, together with the other apostles, have proclaimed to you, with Jesus himself holding the whole household together. In him we are held together in unity, joined together in love and connected together as family. For we have been created new in Christ, no longer as strangers, but now as brothers and sisters; and God is continuing to draw us all closer together as a family, where he also lives by his Spirit.

I am writing to you in the hope that you too would find as much joy in the good news as I have. Even now I rejoice, whether a free man or in jail for proclaiming the glorious truth. I preach it, regardless of the consequences, for the sake of all who have not yet heard it, that they too may know Christ.

Surely you have heard my testimony by now, and the powerful working of God's graceful Spirit in me? God, by his grace, not only saved me, but also revealed to me his eternal plan. It had been a mystery throughout the ages, but has now been revealed through the coming of his Son. This mystery was not revealed to me by a mentor, a rabbi or a theologian, but rather by divine revelation. And so, as you read my letter, you can begin to understand why I so passionately lift Jesus up and seek to make plain the good news of his grace.

How wonderful his eternal plan truly is. The Son of God came down to earth, born of a woman, born under the old covenant of law to fulfil that covenant of law (for it was impossible for anyone else to fulfil it). He brought that first 'exclusive' covenant to a close, in order to establish a new 'inclusive' covenant for all. It is through this divine act of grace that all of mankind, both Jew and Gentile, are now heirs to a relationship with God and equally share in the promise of new life. God is not looking at the nationality of a person, but rather, he is looking at the Christ in one's heart. God has made a way that all mankind may have access to know him through faith in Jesus.

It is this message that I have become a servant to,

according to the gift of God's grace, which continues to work so powerfully in me. And so my boast is solely in Christ, for I have not earned this gift, but have received it through God's love. Indeed, in myself I am truly nothing, less than the least of God's people. If it were based on works I would be given nothing from God. For before my salvation I hated the name of Jesus, tried to destroy the Church, punished Christians and was brutal in my passion against the gospel message. And yet, God has used my life as a testimony to his promise: that in Christ we are made new, clean and without fault in his eyes. My past has truly passed away and I am a new creation in Christ; and so now, in Christ, this grace has been given to me: to proclaim the unsearchable riches of Jesus and to make known the glory of his grace to all mankind; the good news that has been hidden in God's heart since the foundations of the world.

God's purpose is now being outworked through our life together as God's Church, allowing the wisdom of his grace to be revealed to all creation; both here on earth as well as in the heavens above. All this is in accordance with his eternal purpose that has always been grounded and established in the life, and perfect work, of his Son: our Lord Jesus. In Christ, and through faith in him, we may now stand in the very presence of God with absolute freedom and confidence. In light of this wonderful truth, you can understand why it is not a burden for me, or a concern for you, to be imprisoned for preaching the gospel. It is a blessing, not a burden, for me to stand up and proclaim the truth of God's grace, regardless of the consequences.

With all this in mind, I bow before our Father, through whom all of us, as members of his family, receive our name. I pray that God would do wonderful things in you. I'm not suggesting that you attempt to energise yourselves with your own limited strength; rather, my prayer is that God himself, out of his glorious riches may strengthen you with his almighty power, through his Spirit that now lives in you, and that your inner being would be established in his strength. And now, being established in his strength, I pray that you would be able to truly rest in your beloved saviour who dwells in your hearts through faith. By resting in his strength, and trusting in his power, you are also allowing yourself to be rooted and established in his love. Dear family, just as you are established in his grace, I continue to pray that God will work his mighty power in you in order that you may have power, together with everyone in Christ, to grasp how deep his love for all of us truly is.

Oh, I'm telling you the truth; his love is so deep, so wide, so long and so high! The love of Christ has no limits in glory, and all his love is given to us who belong to him. We are the object of his affection, and he delights to reveal to our hearts the depth of his love for us. It is through knowing this love, a love that truly surpasses knowledge, that you may be filled with all that he is.

We belong to him. We are his treasured possession, and as glorious as we know him to be, I can assure you he is even more glorious. Our saviour cannot be measured and he is able to do immeasurably more than all we can ask and imagine. As we come together as the Church, may the revelation of his almighty love and grace be the message that unites us. Let us joyfully thank him together for all we have received through our saviour, Christ Jesus. Of this one thing we can be assured: his love is for us, now and forevermore. Amen.

As a prisoner for the Lord, then, I ask you to always remember the truth of who you are. You are children of the most high God, you are the beloved of Christ, and you are the treasured possession of heaven's king. You are perfect in him, and, with all this in mind, enjoy living a life that reflects this wonderful calling you have received.

Allow the power of God to be active in your life. Be humble and gentle. Remember that we are all still growing in our understanding of God grace, so be patient with one another, allowing God's love to be your guide. As you continue to grow together in the truth of your new covenant reality, allow the Spirit to also lead you in the ways of God's love. We are one body and in all of us there is one Spirit. Likewise, through Christ you were called to one hope, one faith, one united life with Christ; one God and Father of all. It is God's desire that his children would live in unity, so let us be one in spirit as we walk the way of his love together.

As we walk in his love, let us also rejoice that Christ continues to pour out his grace upon all of us, just as he desires. Christ is a gift giver to those who belong to him, just as it says: "When he ascended on high, he led the redeemed in his train, and gave gifts to them." (Now what does 'he ascended' mean, except that he also first came down to earth? Yes, It is Jesus who first descended, and who has now also ascended higher than all the heavens, where his Spirit fills the whole universe!)

It is this very same Jesus who gave some of us to be sent out, with the task of bringing together and encouraging the Church throughout the world, some to share the love of God with words given to them from heaven, some to proclaim the mystery of the gospel now revealed, some to care for the community of God's children and some to teach in accordance with the new covenant truth of God's grace. Some are called in these ways for the benefit of all, my brothers and sisters, that you too would be built up in your calling, and, through faith in the finished work of Christ, would also allow the power of God to work powerfully in you. For no matter what our calling in Christ may be, his purpose remains the same: that we may all be united in the faith and knowledge of the Son of God, and, through accepting his grace and goodness over our lives, to become mature in him, receiving the fullness of his love into our hearts.

Christ loves you completely, and his desire is to give to you the whole measure of his very life in order that you may truly live in him. It is through receiving more of his love, and trusting more in his finished work, completed upon the cross, that you can grow in your faith. God is not measuring you by your works, but by your faith in Jesus, and it is for that reason you can receive a full measure of his love. Faith is not measured by what we do, but by our acceptance and rest in what Christ has already done for us. It is through this truth that we can mature in our faith, no longer being tossed back and forth by all sorts of worldly messages and teachings from men who seek to control us by placing our focus on our works and religious obligations. As children of God we allow our focus to remain on his grace. We walk in the ways of love and speak the truth in love. We are able to do this only because we have full assurance in his love for us. Through this great blessing, we can grow up established in Christ. For it is only through Christ that we can grow in the ways of God, and together, through our faith in Jesus, we can support each other, building each other up in love, just as each one of us outworks God's love in our own life.

So what now? How should we live in light of this wonderful new life we have received in Christ? We should live as Jesus himself lived - as a beloved child of God in the eyes of our Father. We should live by faith, for we know and believe the message of salvation through Jesus is not just a good idea or concept - it is the truth. It is our reality, and now that we live in this wonderful light, we will certainly not live as if we are still in the dark; in the foolishness of a self-adoring lifestyle. A self-adoring lifestyle only leads to darkness, burdens and the hardening of hearts, but a Christ-glorifying lifestyle is led in the light, given rest, and has a heart that is overflowing with hope and love. Those who walk without Christ continue to walk their own way, having lost the 'Christ desire' they were born with (for we have all been made in his image) and having been deceived to accept the 'self-desire' that continues to chase after all the things the body and ego lust after, with a continual desire for more.

You, however, did not come to know Christ according to that pattern. Surely you received the gospel as it truly is: the good news of God's grace that has been given to us in accordance with the truth that is in Jesus. You were taught that Christ became darkness on the cross, so that you may now become light in him. It is not your efforts that have changed you, but rather, the power of the cross. For you traded in all your pain for all his joy, all your brokenness for all his wholeness and all your sins for all his righteousness. You exchanged your old self that was being corrupted by its deceitful desires and were made 'new' in Christ. And now that you are a new person in Jesus, see to it that the attitude of your mind agrees with this glorious reality. God never doubts that you are his beloved, a holy and perfectly loved child, so remind yourself of this truth and enjoy the reality of your new nature. Live in this truth each day, for you have been created new to be like God, full of grace and truth.

Therefore, as you grow in his grace, allow your old mindsets and doubts to be cast aside. The way of love does not speak in the language of lies, but in the language of truth, and so speak truthfully to each other, after all, we are a family and all belong to the one body of Jesus. "In your anger do not fall into unbelief": my dear friends, we all still live in this earthly body, and if, on occasion, your negative emotions overtake you, don't allow them to remain the leader of your life. For you are children of faith, and so remain in this faith and let peace be restored to you. Don't allow frustration to take advantage of your anger and so get a foothold in your life. You have traded in the old for the new, the darkness for the light, and the lies of this world for the truth of God. With this in mind, allow your new life to mirror this reality. If anyone has lived the life of dishonesty, don't continue in that pattern of life; rather, enjoy the empowerment God has now given you to walk in freedom and honesty. In light of this reality, allow yourselves the blessing of being an honest man who can provide not only for himself, but also for those around him. Christ has set us free, be free then, and do something productive with the gifts and abilities God has given you, that you may be a blessing to those in need.

Don't speak in ways that are unwholesome, but as you truly are, speak in ways that reflect your life in Christ. Talk to each other in ways that are helpful in building each other up in love, so that your words may benefit those who listen. The Holy Spirit is now living in you, so remind yourself of his wonderful presence in your life, and, in accordance with his leading, empty yourself of any remaining bitterness, rage and anger. Allow the full work of the Spirit to heal and refresh your inner being so that you may be kind and compassionate to one another. Keep the great work of Christ fresh in your hearts, and forgive one another just as you remember how much Christ has forgiven you.

Keep the eyes of your heart upon Jesus, and allow the working of God's power in you to outlive his love in your daily life. Just as you are dearly loved children, live a life of love. Allow the Holy Spirit to remind you daily just how much Christ loves you and how he gave himself up for you, enabling you to forever stand in the presence of your heavenly Father with freedom and confidence.

You now live in the reality of God's nature of love, and so continue to walk in his way of love and do not chase after the things that are along other darkened paths. The way of love is not sexual immorality, impurity or greed; indeed these things should have no partnership with your life as a child of God. Neither should you fill up your time with foolish talk or dirty jokes; instead, allow your words to result in thanksgiving to God. God's kingdom is one of love, and those who indulge in the immoral and impure things of this world have not yet crossed over into God's kingdom. Don't let anyone deceive you with empty words, for your salvation is not empty of power, but powerful enough to free you from all the things that deceive and trap those still walking along darkened paths. For although you were once in darkness, you have now become light in the Lord. Live as children of light (for the fruit of light is consistent with all goodness and truth) and enjoy walking the path of light that pleases the Lord. Do I really need to tell you what the fruitless deeds from the darkened paths are? I don't think so, for you yourself know the depth of their darkness and why we no longer entangle our lives in such things. For it is shameful to even mention what takes place in darkness. You, however, have traded in your dark secrets for all of God's light. You have been redeemed. Your dirty rags have been removed by the Spirit of God and have been replaced with God's own robe of righteousness. Now that you live in the light your eyes can see what is consistent with the ways of his love and what is not; for his light makes everything visible. That is why it is said: "Wake up, O sleepy one, rise from your unbelief and the light of Christ will shine on you."

Be aware then how you are living. Not as one willfully living in ignorance, but as one who has come to know the truth. Make the most of every opportunity to live in the light, for these days are corrupt. Take the time to understand what the Lord's will is. Don't become disheartened and turn to excessive drinking, which only leads you off the path of light onto the shadows of disillusionment. Instead, be filled with the Spirit of God. Talk with one another with loving affection, with the words found in the Psalms, with hymns and songs that remind you of God's faithfulness. Allow the joy of the gospel to play a heavenly symphony in your hearts to the Lord. As you walk with God, give thanks to him for everything, and do it all in the name of our Lord Jesus. Love one another as you remember Christ's unending love for you.

Wives, believe your husbands when they speak words of loving affection over your life, just as you do with the Lord. For your husband is committed to being a strength to you, as he imitates how Christ is the strength of the Church, his body, whom he loves more than his own life. Now just as we, the Church, submit to Christ when he confirms his love for us, so also wives should submit to their husbands and accept their husbands' praises in everything.

Husbands, love your wives, just as Christ loves his Church and gave himself up for her, declaring her holy, speaking words of life over her regarding her beauty and cleanness; reminding her that she may stand confident of his love as a radiant bride, without stain or wrinkle, or any other blemish; pro-claiming she is his beloved, pure and blameless. In the same way, tell your wives how loved they are, how radiant they are and how beautiful they are in your eyes. Remember how the Lord sees you with the eyes of his grace, and do the same with your wife. Care for your wife as you imitate how Christ cares so abundantly for his church. Scripture declares: *"The day will come when a man will leave his parents in order to enter into a new covenant with his wife, and the two, in the eyes of God, will then become one."* My brothers, this is a profound mystery—but this scripture is talking about Christ and the Church! It is true that in the eyes of God you have been united as *'one'* with your wife through your covenant marriage. What a profound revelation to realise that even your marriages are a glorious illustration given to you from above to help you understand your heavenly reality that, through your union to Jesus, you too have become one with Jesus in the eyes of our Father! And so, as husband and wife, in light of the loving acceptance you have received from Christ, and with the same spirit of love, respect each other as you live together under his care.

Young children, you too have the Spirit of God, and so you too can walk in the ways of love and be obedient to your parents in the Lord, for this is pleasing to God. Indeed, we are all children of the promise of Jesus, and because of this we not only honour our Father in Heaven, but also our parents here in earth.

Fathers, may our Father fill you with the grace of his character, so that you may be an example to your children of the grace and kindness of God. Bring your children up with the example of love, so that they may continue to grow in their own relationship with their heavenly Father.

No matter where you work, or what your tasks are, do them with respect and sincerity of heart. Just as you joyfully obey Christ, so also do what honours your employer. Allow God to work through you, so that you may work wholeheartedly, as if you were serving the Lord, not men. Christ is with you, he loves you, and when you allow his grace to flow through you in your workplace, he will reward you.

To those who are employers, treat your employees with the same respect and sincerity of heart you desire from them. Do not threaten them, for you know that Christ never threatens you, and yet the result is obedience and a fruitful life, so too when you treat your employees with respect and in the spirit of love they will work more productively, to your benefit.

Finally to all of you, be sure to always find your strength in the Lord and in his mighty power. God has equipped you with all you need to stand strong and victorious in Christ. Always remember you are standing not just near Jesus, but you are standing in him. With this in mind, be assured that you can stand against the pressure to conform to the patterns of this world. For we, who are in Christ, do not struggle against people, but against the spirit of deception and the spiritual authorities that try to impose it upon mankind. Therefore put on the full armour of God, so that when the spiritual forces try to deceive you, you may be able to stand your ground, and after you have remained standing in the truth that is found in Christ, you can glory in God, that he is mighty to save. Stand firm then, with the belt of truth buckled around your waist. With the breastplate of Christ's righteousness in place, and with your feet fitted with the readiness to proclaim the goodness of God that comes out of being established in the gospel of his grace and peace. In addition to all this, always keep hold of your mighty shield of faith; not faith in your own godliness, but faith in the perfect redeeming work of Christ, so that any accusation brought against you based on your limitations and weaknesses will be extinguished by the all empowering truth of God's grace before they can even draw near to you. And pray in the Spirit on all occasions with any kind of prayer and request you may have, for your Father will always listen when you call to him. With this in mind, keep your conversation going with the Lord; and don't limit your conversation with him to matters concerning only your own needs, but also discuss the needs of your fellow brothers and sisters in the Lord and express the confidence you have in him, that he will surely meet their needs with the fullness of his grace.

Finally, pray also for me, that the Spirit of God will continue to proclaim his glorious gospel powerfully through me. Pray that when I open my mouth words may be given to me in order that I may also stand firm and passionately proclaim the mystery of the gospel. Pray that I will preach it fearlessly in order that those who hear my message will also believe and enter into a united life with God, embraced in his eternal nature of love. Pray that I may present this truth with all God's power at work in me, just as indeed I should.

Tychicus, my fellow preacher and a faithful servant in the Lord, who has delivered this letter to you, can continue to tell you everything concerning my situation. May he be a blessing to your community as he continues to proclaim the glorious gospel of our saviour Jesus and encourages you in your journey of faith.

May the Lord of all peace pour out his peace upon all of you, along with his love and faith that comes from the very heart of our heavenly Father and the Lord Jesus. Grace to all who love our Lord Jesus Christ with a love that will last throughout eternity.

PHILIPPIANS

PHILIPPIANS

From Paul and Timothy, servants of the greatest message ever proclaimed: the good news that God is not holding our sins against us, but rather, is graceful and mighty to save.

To all the believers in Jesus at Philippi, together with your fellow brothers and sisters among you who have been graced to oversee your communal life together: grace and peace to you all from God our Father who pours out his grace upon you without restraint through our Lord Jesus Christ.

My siblings in Christ, before I say another word, I just have to tell you how much I love you all. Oh, I'm telling you the truth, I find myself filled with joy and spontaneously thanking our God every time

I simply remember you. I'm full of hope and happiness whenever I pray about you all, because I know how you have always stood with me in our mutual faith and commitment in God's gospel. The gospel that declares God is love, God is gracious, and God has made a way to freely reconcile all of mankind to himself by faith in his Son apart from any other requirements. Your partnership in the gospel is so comforting, for, although there are those who reject the reality of God's radical good news, you have embraced it from the first day you heard it until now.

And so, knowing that you are planted in the truth of God's gospel, I am fully confident that all the good works God has begun in you will also be brought to completion. More than that, I'm certain that he will continue to outwork his loving ways in you until the day we see Jesus once more. It's only natural that I feel this way about you, for I hold you all in my heart. I am fully aware of how dearly loved you are by our wonderful Lord Jesus, and I too love you with all of God's love that abounds within me. And just as I hold you in my heart, I know that you too hold me in yours. It makes no difference what my circumstances are, whether I am chained hand and foot, or freely standing up for the defence of the gospel and passionately confirming the truth of God's eternal love, I know that all of you share in God's grace with me; and you know how much I love you. I'm not just trying to flatter you with words; God himself can testify how much loving affection I have in my heart regarding you all.

My friends, with the fullness of this God-given love for all of you, this is my heart's desire for you: that your love may continue to not only overflow, but abound with even more knowledge and understanding in regards to the nature of God, so that you may walk in his ways of love and discern, without needing to be told, what God desires and what he loves. I pray this for you, so you may be blessed with a life that reflects the truth of your present reality: that you truly are holy and blameless. I eagerly desire that you may be blessed, abundantly blessed, as you witness God outworking his ways of love in and through you until the day we see Jesus once more. We now walk with him, and we rejoice that we see him with the eyes of our heart each new day. What is more, the day is coming when we shall also see him face to face; oh, what a glorious day that shall be. And, until then, I am convinced your lives will be filled with the fruit of Jesus; for it is Jesus in us who is producing the fruit of heaven in us and he will continue to bless our hearts with the outworking of a fruitful life, to the glory and the praise of God.

I want you to be assured that my imprisonment is not something to feel burdened or anxious about. For it has all turned out to serve my heart's desire for the gospel to continue advancing. I rejoice, even in what I am currently suffering, for I see how more and more people are accepting the reality of God and the truth of his grace.

Oh, how wonderful to see people not only coming to an understanding, but truly accepting God's incredible gift of new life in Christ. Indeed, the whole palace guard is aware I am not a criminal. They realise I am an ambassador for the incredible good news from God; the good news that is for all of mankind. It's not only those who have been ordered to guard me who understand I am in chains for Jesus, but actually everyone knows it. In fact, although I was placed in chains to silence the message of the gospel, my chains have only encouraged the brothers in the Lord to proclaim the gospel message even more courageously and fearlessly. Ha! It just proves that a man can be chained and silenced, but the message of God's abundant grace and love cannot!

I know that you are just as aware as I am that not everyone's motivation for preaching is pure; but you should also be assured that there are many who have the right motivation to preach. The latter are partnering with me, preaching God's good news despite facing the same opposition to the message of grace that originally placed me in prison. They know I am in chains for the message of God's new life, new covenant and a new hope available to all.

The former are more interested in their own reputation than they are in the message of God's grace; attempting to discredit my own ministry from their self-appointed positions that they have created for themselves.

But what does it matter? The most important thing is that Christ is being preached. Sometimes from false motives, and sometimes from true, but in every way Christ is preached. I rejoice that our glorious Lord and saviour is being preached. Oh, how pleasing it is to my spirit to know the testimony of Jesus is being proclaimed, and so, whether from impure or pure motives, I rejoice and am greatly delighted in my heart.

I rejoice, and I will continue to do so, for God is winning the battle in his eternal plan to rescue mankind from the lie enslaving the world and liberating them into the truth the gospel declares. With this in mind I am full of joy and confidence. What is more, I am greatly encouraged that because of your heart of love, that cries out to God for my well-being, together with the help that the Spirit gives me, what has happened to me will not ruin me, but rather it will be turned around by the powerful love of God for my deliverance.

I am full of hope and I eagerly expect that when I stand before the authorities here I will not fall into weakness and conceal the gospel, but rather, that God would give me the sufficient courage I need to hold up the good news for all to see, and that Christ himself would be powerfully revealed in me and lifted high, as indeed he should be; whether that be through my release or my execution.

For to me, life is not defined by living, but by my united life with Jesus, and death does not bring my life to an end, but releases me to see Christ face-to-face and finally live in the fullness of glory with him. If I am released from prison I will continue, through the grace of God, in preaching his message and will surely be blessed to witness his message bearing fruit in the lives and hearts of those who accept it. But what do I truly desire? I honestly don't know! My heart is torn, for although I long to be with Jesus in glory, which is better by far, I also long to continue this walk of faith with you all, and as I ponder this thought, in my heart I realise it's more necessary for you that I do remain in the body. In fact, I'm already now convinced of this, and for this reason I know that Christ won't take me home just yet, but rather, I will remain for your benefit. I'm sure that I will continue with you all, helping you to see more of God's loving-kindness and, through the power at work in the message of God's grace, establish you more and more in his nature and identity, which is also your identity in Christ. I'll stay for your progress and joy in the faith, so that your joy in Christ may abound and overflow on account of me, and my joy may also abound because God has granted me the blessing of being with you all once more; for you know how much I love you.

Whatever ends up happening, allow your life to be conducted in a way that reflects into the world around you the inner reality you are experiencing through the gospel of Jesus. Let your life reflect the abundance of grace, love and kindness you have freely received through the gospel. In doing this, not only will the light of love touch those around you, but also I will know that you are standing firm in the reality of your new creation life in Jesus. For although we had many separated lives before we entered into Christ, now in Christ we are one. Let yourselves therefore live in this divine unity, standing firm as one united spirit, taking your stand as one man for faith of the gospel without being afraid of those who oppose you. For as much as the gospel is glorious, it is also an offense to those who would rather hold to their false belief in a lifeless god, a brutal god or an angry god than accept the truth that God is defined by his life, his love and his abundant grace. Stand firm therefore in your acceptance of God's true nature and identity, even in the face of slander and opposition, and let the very nature of God's life, love and grace shine abundantly. This will be evidence to those who are lost in their own religious obsession with the notion of an angry God that there is a way for man to be rescued from such destructive theology and be saved into the truth of God's love. For your lives testify that God loves and God saves, and all of this by grace; not by worldly will power, but rather by the divine power of Christ at work in you.

We know that Christ himself was rejected because he revealed to mankind the truth regarding God. He presented God in his divine and heavenly reality, and the religious and secular world alike rejected him because of it. We have not only been granted the joy of believing in Jesus, but also of being truly united with him, even suffering the same rejection he suffered because we too now stand up for the truth of God's eternal nature of grace and love, apart from any religious traditions and obligations. All who join us in our stand for the gospel not only partake in the joy of the gospel, but also the struggle. And so now you too participate in this struggle, just as I had the same kind of struggle while I was living amongst you, and, in fact, as you now hear, I continue to have.

And so now, just as your soul has found its rest in your united life with Christ, and you have also taken your stand in this divine reality, allow the outworking of your daily actions to also be defined and empowered from this united life. I know how much all of you have been encouraged through being made new into the very body and life of Christ, how comforted you now are from his love and how you have all been filled with compassion through his life. So now, make my heart also rejoice by having that same love for one another. God has graciously softened our hearts with his love, so that we too can participate in his divine desire of pouring out heaven's love into the lives of others. Let us allow the love that God has so abundantly poured into our lives also overflow freely into the lives of those around us with great joy; and let us do this with one heart, as we now walk in unity, being one in spirit and purpose.

Don't seek a life that is driven by self-focused ambition, but rather, allow the ambition of Christ to drive you; for it is Christ in you who is ambitious to love, to show grace and to help others in their weaknesses. And so, just as you are one with Christ, allow yourselves the joy of participating in his divine ambition and be open and aware of the needs and interests of others around you.

We are truly one with God, his beloved children and inheritors of all that is his. Now, let us enjoy this reality, not using our identity to belittle those around us or to exalt ourselves, puffing ourselves up in our minds and believing that we should be treated like gods in this world. It's true that we are one with God, but let us look to our saviour as our example of how to live in light of this glorious reality. For although we have been made one with God, our attitude should be the same as that of Christ Jesus:

For Jesus was in every way God, and yet he did not consider his divine reality something he needed to grasp. He didn't desire to parade around as the all powerful deity, but rather he stripped himself of all his heavenly glory, and made himself nothing. He was still one with God, but he volunteered to take on the nature of a servant and be made in human likeness. He was one with God, and yet was willing to be found in the appearance of a man; he chose to humble himself for the benefit of those who were weak, lost and broken. He chose to die that they may be strong, found and whole; even at such a cost as to die on a cross!

And what was the result of such love, such humility, and such confidence in his true identity through it all? Our heavenly Father exalted him to the highest place in all of eternity, and gave him a name more honoured than any name; the name of Jesus. It is Jesus, who, through the revelation of his unending love and sacrifice, will draw all men into the reality of his loving kindness. It is because of his willingness to humble himself and first serve all of mankind, that all of mankind will come to see the truth of Christ, understand the depths of his humili-ty, and come to accept his divine identity. The love of Christ will succeed in bringing all of mankind to bow their knee before his great throne, each freely declaring that Jesus Christ is Lord; and as each individual acknowledges the way of salvation is received not by works, but by the grace of God, our Almighty God will truly receive all the glory!

In the light of this wonderful reality, let us freely and voluntarily walk in the same pattern as the one we have been united with forever. We are now walking this earth as sons and daughters of God, and yet, just like Jesus, we chose not to lord this reality over others; rather, we follow his example and take on the nature of servants. We don't derive our identity from the world; rather, we are free to serve the world through God's love because we are already secure in our divine identity in Christ.

Therefore, my dear friends, we have been made heirs of heaven, but also called to be servants to mankind. With this in mind, continue to work out this great salvation with awe and amazement, for it is a radical reality; a heavenly gift that the Spirit will continue to establish you in as you walk with him. Your salvation in Christ is assured, and the Spirit of God will continue to shine the light of this truth into your hearts and minds, and also empower you to live a life in the same pattern as Jesus, full of grace and truth. It is the Spirit of God who worked powerfully in Jesus while he walked the earth, and that very same Spirit now works in you to live, to desire and to act in accordance with God's desires and purposes.

Allow the Spirit to remind you of the truth, that you are beloved heirs of heaven and have been made blameless and pure, children of God who are free to live in the light of his love. Although the world is cracked and corrupted, it cannot break God's children, for we have been made new in Christ without fault, and with the express purpose of shining the love of God into this broken generation. So rest in his love, do everything without complaining or arguing, and allow his love to shine through you; for there is no greater light than the light of God's love, and that love abides in you. How wonderful is our reality, that God has chosen us to be a light in the world, like stars in the universe. Continue, therefore, to hold out the way of Jesus; the ways of his love, and bless my heart in doing so. For my greatest joy is seeing you stand firm in your belief in God's good news. Indeed, I look forward to boasting on the day I see Jesus once more that you truly lived in the reality of the gospel, your new nature and your divine inheritance.

I am in chains for the gospel you are now living out, and I rejoice to hear of your faith and assurance in the gospel, just as you should rejoice and be glad with me, for my chains only bind my body, but in my spirit I am as free as Christ himself, to the glory of God.

I am hopeful that God will create the way for me to send Timothy to you soon, for I long to hear news about you, and I'm sure that when I do my heart and spirit will be greatly refreshed. You know how dear Timothy is to me; I have no one else like him. He loves you all with the same affection I do, and his interests are not focused on himself, but rather in your well-being. For it seems everyone has set their focus on their own interests, instead of the interests of Jesus. However, you know that Timothy has laboured alongside me, like a son with his father, as we worked to present and defend the most glorious of all messages: the gospel of God's grace. So I hope to send Timothy to you soon, and he also desires to visit you, but we first need to wait and see how things go with me. However, as I have already stated, I'm confident in the Lord that I will be released, and when I am, I will also come to visit you all.

I feel it's also necessary to send Epaphroditus back to you. He is a brother, a co-worker and a fellow soldier. I'm so thankful that you sent him to me to take care of my needs, and indeed he has done just that. His heart is full of love not only for me, but also for all of you, and he longs for all of you. In fact, as you know he was very ill, and almost died, but God was merciful to him, and also to me too, sparing me the sorrow of losing such a wonderful friend. He is back to full health now, and I am eager to send him back to you, that you can see him once more and be filled with joy at his well-being, and I too can relax knowing that you have been reunited with him. Welcome him warmly when he returns, and honour him, for he put his life on the line while he was here in Rome, helping me in all the ways you too would have helped me, if you had had the opportunity.

And so, just as we are a united family in Jesus, enjoy your united life with Jesus and rejoice in him. I know I say this a lot, but it really cannot be said enough. It's a joy to write it, and it's also a healthy reminder for you. It does our hearts good to remember Jesus and the covenant of grace we have with him. Remind yourself of the depths of this love for you, and the inheritance that is yours in him. Rejoice in the reality of every good thing you have received through being made one with him. It is through remembering Jesus that the love of God refreshes us and the weight of the world is removed from our shoulders.

Watch out for those who desire to yoke you to religion. They are zealous for their own distorted ideas of what a follower of Jesus should be like, and will even try to use the name of Jesus, as well as taking Scripture out of context, to promote their false, religious perspectives. They love to establish their own form of religion, of which they lord their 'spiritual authority' over people. However, they purposely disregard the fact that Jesus did not come to start another religion, but to fulfill an old one! He now offers all mankind a covenant of grace that is based on his love and finished work upon the cross; not based on mankind's observance of religious practices and obligations. We, who are in Christ, are truly free to live and commune with God and one another in spirit and in truth. We have had our hearts made new with the nature of Christ, and the old nature has been cut away by the Spirit of God. We don't put our confidence in what we do to prove ourselves faithful to God; we put our confidence in Christ, who has proved God's faithfulness to us. Religion will promote confidence in our outward performance in life, but we maintain that our confidence is inward. Our confidence is in the reality that Christ, our hope of glory, lives in us.

The reason I passionately place my full confidence in the reality of Christ in me is not because I have nothing I could boast about in regards to my own works. On the contrary, I could boast more than any man about my religious accomplishments in the flesh. In fact, according to a life devoted to God through religious acts, I was practically perfect. I was born into the right religion, passed through all the ceremonial rites of passage my religion required, I held to the strictest form of all the laws and spiritual disciplines my religion demanded of me. In fact, if someone were to judge me based on a legalistic, works based understanding of being a 'godly' person I would have been found faultless. But boasting in our religious or 'godly' accomplishments goes against the truth of the gospel; for life with God isn't defined by how perfectly one can fulfil laws and religious requirements, but rather by God's grace to fulfil all requirements on our behalf so we can rest and walk with him. And so I consider the religious zeal I once had a loss, I could even go so far as to say I consider it rubbish; even if others around would gladly consider it to their credit, I consider it a loss. I think this way because I know God has offered me a far greater reality: the reality that Christ is in me, and the opportunity to know him as a saviour, a friend and a brother; to be one with him in perfect love and acceptance apart from any religious performance or self-imposed requirements. I long to know him more, and I desire to see myself in him. I want to see myself in the mirror of his perfection, and not in the mirror of religious obligations that can only reflect my poor attempts of earning a right standing before God. The mirror of Christ allows me to see the truth: that my right standing before God is by faith in all that Christ has accomplished on my behalf.

I want to know Christ, and this is exactly what God offers us freely, as a gift to all who freely receive it: the gift to know him. Like you, I've taken hold of this great blessing and simply refuse to trade it in for knowing merely a religious formula. I desire to know Christ and grow in my understanding of just how powerful his resurrection truly was and how the ongoing effects of that glorious moment continues to impact my life and the lives of all mankind. I want to know all of Christ, not only the moments of his triumphs; I also want to identify with him in his suffering. For Christ himself suffered rejection by those whose agenda was to defend their religion and protect their own self-appointed religious authority. They even went so far in their zeal as to despise the living God they claimed to believe in. As for me, I want to walk with Jesus, and identify with him. I want to experience the heavenly acceptance that comes through uniting myself with him, even at the expense of suffering rejection by the religious zealots who so fiercely oppose the message of God's grace. I desire to be free in Christ's love, empowered by his Spirit and ultimately live forever in his resurrection.

Our united life in Christ is so glorious, and I know I still have more to discover and receive. I'm aware that my spirit, as a new creation, has been made perfect in Christ, but my body is still awaiting its redemption and is burdened by its imperfections. Regardless, I move forward with my full confidence in Christ, for that is the reason Christ took hold of me. My beloved siblings in Christ, I can openly say I face moments of weakness, but I am not ashamed, for my hope is not in my perfect strength, but rather it is in the perfect strength of Jesus. And so I do this one thing: I forget about the past, including both my successes and failures. I leave them all in the past and I lay hold of a far more glorious future, one that is defined by my faith in Christ. For my life is now defined by my identity in Christ. I have already joyfully been made a new creation in my spirit, and I continue heavenward in this faith walk to one day also receive the gift of a new creation body.

All of us who are mature in Christ should take such a view of things. If you disagree, don't take offence at what I'm writing, but allow the Spirit to speak to you regarding my words, and ask God to make his ways clear to you. In all we do, let's enjoy the divine identity that we have already attained in Christ and also allow Christ in us to shine this nature of love and grace into the world around us as we journey from glory to glory together.

Join with others in following the way of love and grace, for Jesus himself lived a life full of grace and love towards those around him. He is our divine example, it is the example I follow, and it is this example others have seen in my life and the example they have also chosen to live their own lives by. Take note of those in your community who live their life full of love and grace for others, and be encouraged by the light of Christ shining through them.

As I have already explained to you, I'll remind you again now. It is a foolish man indeed who can recite God's laws, but refuses to allow God's way of love to shine through his life. It brings tears to my eyes to know that many who have heard the message of Jesus have only taken hold of it as if it were merely a title to wear, while refusing to step into the full spiritual reality of the gospel. Instead of rejoicing in the completed work of Christ upon the cross, they live as enemies of his grace, choosing to remain yoked to the law that Christ came to free them from. They think this is to their glory, but it is actually to their shame! Their minds are yoked to a worldly understanding of God's kingdom; but our citizenship is in heaven, where our saviour is seated in heavenly places, and it is in him that we place our confidence and await his return in glory. Our hope is in Christ, who, through the very same power that enables him to bring the whole universe under his control, will bless us with what he has promised: a new creation body to house our new creation spirits.

Oh, the glory! He will be faithful to us and transform our lowly, weak bodies so that they will be like his glorious body! Therefore, my family in Christ, you whom I love so much, this is how you can stand firm in the Lord. Keep the eyes of your hearts on your heavenly reality, and allow Christ to shine the light of his love in and through you.

Euodia and Syntyche, my dear sisters, just as you are ambassadors for the gospel of peace, live at peace with one another. I also ask all of you in Philippi to help these amazing women, for they have worked alongside me, along with Clement and the rest of my fellow workers, for the sake of making the gospel known. The gospel is not a message of man's obligations to God, but the divine message of God's faithfulness to man: that he made a way for all of us to enter into his eternal intention of a covenant of grace. Indeed, it is through God's amazing grace that our names have been written in the book of life. What a glorious life we have received in him.

Oh, how we can rejoice! Yes, I'm aware that I'm in chains, and my body is wearing away, but the gospel cannot be chained and my spirit is being renewed every day. It is in light of this great reality that I say again: rejoice! Allow the graceful and gentle character of Christ in you to be evident to all, for he is living in you. Don't fall captive to the fear of the unknown, don't let the uncertainties of tomorrow burden your hearts with anxiety, but rather, take hold of your divine reality. Talk with God about all your needs, not from a place of fear, but rather from a place of trust and thanksgiving, for he understands and he loves you deeply. He is our peace and he will guard our hearts and minds in times of trouble and difficulties. The world attempts to force its weight of worry upon us, but it is our God, who transcends worldly understanding, who will allow his peace, love and faith to reign in us to the glory of God.

And so, let your hearts and minds find their focus upon whatever is following the ways of love and truth; yes, let your minds ponder upon all that is noble, pure, lovely and admirable. Set your thoughts on all the things that you see God's character shining through, for he is moving within everything that is praiseworthy and full of love. Follow the way of love. This is the goal of my life: to live according to the pattern of God's nature, full of grace and love. So, take note also of my way of life, follow the ways of God's love and enjoy the gift of God's peace that he will continue to fill you with as you journey this life together with him.

I rejoice in the goodness of God, and I also rejoice greatly to know how much concern you have for me; indeed, I know that you have always been concerned for my well-being, but you did not have the opportunity to show it. I am blessed to see how much loving affection you hold in your hearts for me. I am blessed; blessed by God for his peace, regardless of my circumstances, and blessed by you for your heart of love that shines towards me in my difficult circumstances.

I am a blessed man indeed, for I have learned, through resting in the love and grace of God, the secret of having a life that is content in every situation. I have been both free and in chains, well-fed and hungry, living in plenty and living in want. I have experienced a life that had need of nothing, and a life that had nothing but need. Yet, no matter what the circumstances are on the outside, I live with the inner revelation that Christ is always with me, he knows me, he holds me, and he loves me. I am truly united with Jesus. I'm in him, and he is in me. I'm secure in his embrace, and he is faithful to his promise to never leave me. And so, with such a glorious spiritual reality, I have discovered that my temporal circumstances and worldly burdens don't change my place of contentment in Christ. I can live, enjoy, and rejoice in all circumstances through my united life with Christ, who gives me strength.

Not only does Christ comfort me, but he also works through you to comfort me. I am greatly comforted to see how your heart's desire was to help me; even going so far as to share in my troubles. You're all aware of the situation I faced in the days you first came to accept and put your trust in the gospel. I travelled with the sole intention of testifying to the good news of God's grace, and although many were encouraged by my life and message, none of the believers felt moved to support me in my ministry, except you. You have supported me time and time again; whenever I have needed help, and I rejoice in the Lord that you once again have it upon your hearts to support me now. It's not that I desire a gift from you, but rather, I am grateful that you can share in the preaching of the gospel with me. From a worldly perspective you are crediting my account, but from a heavenly perspective it is God who is crediting yours; and because of this I rejoice.

As for me, I have more than enough now that I have received your generous gifts of support from Epaphroditus. My heart is blessed by your love for me; your support is a comfort to me and a blessing in the work I'm doing here, so thank you my dear friends. I know that just as you have given from a heart of grace to meet my needs, our God will move from his heart of grace to meet all of your needs according to the abundant resources he has stored up in Christ Jesus. So, let us continue to walk in awe of our God and rejoice as we see him working in and through us; may he receive all the glory for ever and ever.

Please pass on my greetings to all the beloved saints in Christ Jesus, just as the brothers here with me send you their greetings. God has drawn many into his heavenly family here in Rome. Those who belong to Caesar's household, and, by the grace of God, now all the more to God's household, also send you greetings. May the grace of Jesus be with

you, bless you, and keep you strong in his grace. Let
it be.

COLOSSIANS

COLOSSIANS

Paul, singled out by God to proclaim the truth of his divine love for mankind that is now understood through the grace of his Son Jesus. Together with Timothy our brother. To my faith-filled brothers and sisters in Colossae, set apart and made alive in the endless love of Christ; grace and peace to you in abundance from our heavenly Father.

We are always thanking God, our eternal Father, for you all. Indeed, ever since we received news of your faith, and the love you have for each other, we have been filled with joy and continue to thank God over and over that you have received the light of life. What a blessing it is for all of us to finally understand the truth: that God considers us so valuable he allowed his Son to die for us, in order that we can now live eternally with him. We have such significance in the eyes of the Almighty.

I must say, it truly is a joy to hear of your faith, and how God is working powerfully within your community. A faith that has arisen through your understanding of God's love for you and the acceptance of your glorious inheritance, stored up for you in heaven. Oh, how 'good' the 'news' truly is. God has established a covenant for us based on his nature, his love, and his divine grace.

We no longer need to live distant from him, scared of him, or ashamed before him. We no longer strive to relate with him based on our limited strength and faithfulness; rather, through a glorious act of his grace, our new covenant is based on his divine strength and his perfect ability to be faithful to us. We have entered into a covenant with God that isn't sealed with our imperfect sacrifices, but rather, with the perfect sacrifice of Christ. How incredible to know that the covenant we have now received was not sealed with the blood of men, nor the blood of animals, but with the blood of Christ. He did everything on our behalf, so that God could now freely give to us as a gift all the benefits of Christ's perfect finished work.

That gift, my friends, is the gospel: the good news that God has now established his very own nature in you. That is what his grace is my friends. It is the very nature of God. It's not just a nice word, or a theoretical doctrine – it's real. It's alive in you! Grace is God's divine, empowering nature of love.

How wonderful to know that you have now been established in God's grace. Christ in you is the gift of God, and he lives passionately in you now. You freely and joyfully received him through the word of truth: the gospel of unfailing love that has come to you.

God has made it possible for the whole world to be set free from spiritual slavery, and now desires to lead all of mankind into a whole new spiritual reality. All over the world people are being set free from lies, fear, pain, sin, hopelessness, shame, guilt and condemnation and entering into a reality of truth, love, hope, peace and joy. I know you can testify to this reality, for these very things have been happening in your community since the first day you heard the gospel and understood God's grace in all its truth.

How wise God is. How amazing his ways. That freedom from bondage would not come through man's determination and will power, but rather, through the understanding of his grace. You learned the good news from Epaphras, our fellow preacher, who, with a passion and joy, proclaimed the gospel of Christ to you just as we would have, had we been with you. He has just arrived to visit us and has told us of your love in the spirit.

We really have been blessed to hear of your faith; indeed, we have not stopped praying for you ever since the day we heard about you. We pray that

God, our loving Father, would pour into your hearts such an abundant revelation of his love that it may result in you having a clearer understanding of his will. As you know, it is because of the great promise you have in Christ that you no longer need a law, or any other written principles to understand God's will. What you need, my dear friends, is the very thing you have been given: his Holy Spirit living in you! And now, just as his Holy Spirit lives in you, we pray that he will continue to speak to you with all heavenly wisdom and understanding. For we desire to see in you the same results that you also desire: that you may be empowered through the Spirit of God to live a life that reflects God's love; for we know how much you identify with God's love, and we can testify how much this makes God smile.

As you enjoy the journey of walking with God, allow him the joy of revealing to your spirit more understanding regarding the finished work of Christ upon the cross. The more you understand this, the more you will experience faith growing in you. God's grace will enable you to trust more in his power, stay in his rest and live by his Spirit. It is through knowing the greatness of Christ, not a theory, but a living reality, and allowing our minds to also accept this wonderful reality that God himself gains more access to strengthen us according to his glorious might. We can assure you that it is God himself who will strengthen you to live a life of great endurance and patience. What will the result of this blessed life be? It will surely result in all of us continually coming into the throne room of God and thanking him for all he has done for us. Jesus' life not only redeems us; his life also qualifies us to share in the inheritance of heaven. For it was God almighty, our great king, who rescued us from the world controlled by deception and darkness, and, by his power, brought us into the kingdom of light. That kingdom is founded in his Son Jesus Christ. It is in Christ that we have redemption, acceptance, an inheritance and the profound grace of having our sins forgiven forever!

We have everything because we belong to the One who truly is everything. I tell you the truth, and let us never grow tired of meditating on this wonderful truth: Jesus truly is everything! He is the Way, the Truth, the Life, the Light and the Day! He is the Peace of God, the Word of God and the Love of God. He is the Alpha and the Omega, the Beginning of eternity and the End of eternity. He is literally God himself: the very image of the invisible God. He is the DNA of God that brought to life all of creation and it is through his life that all things were created. He is before all things, and in him all things hold together. In regards to our redemption, he has done it all. He is the eternal high priest and the eternal sacrificial lamb; the God and the man. He both *made* the sacrifice for our redemption and *was* the sacrifice for our redemption. He has no limits in power, no limits in authority and no limits in his love for us! He is the Almighty, the glory of God, and the head of his body, the Church. He has made us one with him, just as a head is one with its body, so too are we now one with Christ. We have become one with '*the One*' in whom everything finds its purpose and origins.

The eternal Father was pleased that his Son would have all his fullness dwell in him. Jesus is the creator of all things, so that all created things may once more be reconciled to God through him. His majesty is beyond understanding, and yet it can be seen in its fullness when we look to the cross of Christ. It was upon the cross that this almighty, universe creating Son of God was killed by the hands of his own creation. It was upon the cross that his perfectly pure blood was shed for our sins. It was upon the cross that he proved the unlimited depths of his love for all of mankind. It is this cross that reveals the power of God to reconcile to himself all things, whether things on earth or things in heaven. When we remember who it was that died upon that cross, not just a good man, but the Son of God himself, we can see God as he truly is: the God of all grace who has no limits in his love for us.

At one point in time, we all assumed we had to keep our distance from God; believing, in our minds, that our weaknesses and shameful behaviour made us an enemy of God. But how wrong our thinking was! For the very God we believed was against us actually journeyed from heaven to earth in order to reach out to us with the truth of his eternal love. Oh, what a wonderful revelation of truth: he loves us! For, although we felt a million miles away from God and stained with imperfections, God drew us near to himself through the physical body of his very own Son, who went so far as to die for us, in order that we could be made new in him, and presented before God in his holiness and perfection. We have been granted the privilege of being made completely new with the identity of Jesus before the throne of God, and for that reason we now stand in God's presence with freedom and confidence, without blemish and free from accusation. For we are not seen in our weaknesses and past mistakes, but forever in his grace, cleansed forever by his mercy, and adopted into his very own family as sons and daughters.

My brothers and sisters, it is the reality of God's grace that keeps us in this place of confidence, so don't fall back into believing grace is not enough; for it is when we try to earn our right standing that we fall into all kinds of fear, weakness and unnecessary self-condemnation. Remain in the truth of his grace my friends, and enjoy the confidence that comes from being wrapped in his unfailing love. This is the good news you heard, and the divine reality that you have taken your stand upon. It is the gospel message that fills the whole world with hope, and indeed has already been proclaimed to the whole world, but now made clear through the death, resurrection and new creation life of Christ. God has already proclaimed to all of creation his covenant of peace; a testimony that has now come to fulfilment at its appointed time, for Scripture testifies:

"God said to Noah and his children: "I now establish my covenant with you, and all the generations that come after you; and indeed, I proclaim it to every part of my creation. Yes, I establish this covenant of peace with all of creation, with every living creature in the entire world. This is an everlasting covenant between me and every living creature on earth. Never again will I inflict judgement; never again will I judge the world. Rather, I make a covenant of salvation; a covenant that will save the world. And I give you a sign to remind you that I will never revoke this covenant; a sign for the generations to come; a sign of the covenant I have established between me and all life on earth."

That sign, my fellow brothers and sisters, was a rainbow, a shadow that represented the eternal sign of Christ's cross that now reminds God forever to shine his favour and grace to all of us. Indeed, Isaiah confirms that the covenant God established in the days of Noah was in the same pattern as his eternal covenant of grace now established by the finished work of Jesus; as it is written:

> "'To me, this new covenant I make now is like in the time of Noah, when I promised the punishment of Noah would never be repeated. So now I have made an eternal oath, a promise I will not turn back on. I promise never to be angry with you again, and never to rebuke you again. Although the strongest of things in the world may be shaken, and the stable found-ations of the world may crumble, yet my unfailing love for you will never be shaken, nor will my covenant of peace ever be removed,' says the King of heaven, the father of compa-ssion and the God of all grace."

This is the good news that you heard, that indeed has already been divinely proclaimed to every creature under heaven, and the message I am call-ed, and blessed, to continue proclaiming. I am hon-oured to serve mankind with the proclamation of this incredible good news: that God is not counting mankind's sins against them, but rather, he is freely reconciling all by his grace, mercy and love. Praise

God for the reality of his good news to mankind. God has made a way to reconcile us all to himself, because the truth of our past rebellion was 'over-ruled' by the truth of Christ's physical body nailed upon the cross for all of us. He has taken away our shame and has now clothed us with his grace. Our hope is in the redemptive work of Jesus and we are not moved from this position for it is the very hope that is given to us in the gospel.

As you know, I'm in prison for the sake of the gospel. I face rejection and punishment for being bold enough to declare the truth of God's grace. Just as Jesus was rejected for such a proclamation, I freely follow him in both proclaiming the truth as well as suffering, like he did, the rejection of the message and the beating of my body. I do this for the sake of Christ's body, which is the Church. Indeed, I have become a servant to all who are part of the body of Christ. My task is a glorious one that I love and rejoice in, for I consider it the highest honour to present to you the word of God in its fullness. God's word was revealed in a written format from the beginning, but there was still a mystery concealed within it that was kept hidden from all the generations that went before us, but now it has been disclosed to the saints!

It is to the saints, those who have been born-again into the life of Jesus, which God is pleased to make fully known this divine mystery. What is the mystery that past generations could not see in the word of God? It is the reality of Christ in you, the hope of glory. All the Scriptures are testifying about his life, his sufferings and the grace that would come to us through his resurrection. It has now been revealed to you that the word of God is not simply a written code, but it is alive and living in you! The glorious riches of God's word lives in you; Christ in you is the word of God, and he is your hope of glory.

It is Jesus, and the glorious riches of his life in us, that we proclaim, teaching everyone with the wisdom that comes through God's grace, so that you don't put your trust in your imperfect works, but rather, in the perfect finished work of Jesus; and, in doing so, we can present you as truly perfect in Christ. Perfection in God's eyes is a gift to all who put their trust in the work of his Son. It is to this end I labour, sharing God's message with all Christ's energy, which works so powerfully in me.

I want to share with you, my dear family, just how much I am struggling for you all, and also for those in the cities close to you. Not only for those I've had the privilege of meeting personally, but also for those I have not met. My heart is full of love for all of you, for you are all my beloved siblings in Christ.

My struggle is not for my sake, but for yours, my dear family. It is because I'm so passionate about the good news from God that is rightly yours in Christ that I press forward, despite the obstacles and opposition, with the hope that you will be encouraged in heart and united in the abounding love of God. I labour for the sake of this goal, knowing that when we are encouraged in our hearts, and united in our love, a spiritual highway is created that opens up a way for us to travel together into the full riches of divine understanding, leading us in love to accept the mystery of God. That divine mystery is that God is not at all demanding, judgmental or legalistic; he doesn't want to live in a 'temple' or be brought sacrifices. He is truly the divine God who does not desire a religion, but rather, an intimately united life with us all. This mystery has finally come to light now that we see Jesus, for he is the mystery of God made plain to us all.

It is not in God's written word that the full riches of complete understanding are found, but in the fullness of Jesus, who is God's word made alive to us - Christ in you. In him is the full understanding of God's nature and way of love. In Christ are hidden the abounding treasures of God's wisdom and knowledge. I'm reminding you of this so that you won't be easily misled by fine-sounding arguments. You can rest assured that if Christ is in you, and you are in him, then he will open up your heart and mind to walk in God's ways and bless you with the wisdom of God in every circumstance. Although I'm not with you now, my heart is with you and I am delighted to see that your stand is upon the reality of Jesus in your lives and how your faith rests in him.

Now, just as you accepted Jesus as your Lord, the one who has made you perfectly acceptable in every way before your heavenly Father, continue to live in him. He offers us a transformed life that is a glorious and daily experience. Rest in his divine love for you, and, in that place of heavenly rest, allow the Spirit to work as he desires. Live in Christ; allow your life to be rooted in his life that you may also be built up in his grace, strengthened in your knowledge of all he has accomplished for you and abounding in joy and thankfulness that a united life with Christ brings forth.

Keep yourself grounded in this glorious reality, and be on your guard. Don't allow anyone to take you captive through hollow and deceptive ideas. They may sound impressive with their reasoning and philosophy which depends on human traditions, historical research and basic principles of the world, but none of it is based on the reality of Christ.

Christ in you is a mystery that can only be understood by the Spirit of God, and so those without the Spirit will naturally try to explain life, God and faith from a worldly perspective that does not depend on the reality of Christ in you, your hope of glory. Be aware of this, my brothers and sisters, that you may not be so easily enslaved by their worldly teaching. For it is in Jesus that the fullness of the almighty, divine God can be seen and understood, and you have been given Jesus in his fullness. What a blessing! What a glorious reality, that the one who is the fullness of God himself is living in you.

Christ is above every power and authority, there is nothing above his rule, and he is the ruler of our hearts. This is our reality, and in him we understand the reality of all things. Take circumcision for example: the reality of circumcision is not about cutting away the flesh, but rather it is about the work Christ does in the heart of a believer. He is the one that cut away the sinful nature in you in order that the righteous nature could forever shine. You don't have to cut away the sinful nature, it has been done for you by the grace of Christ. What a gift, that we are now free to live for God. Our faith is not merely a theory; it is founded in a profound reality.

The truth is we were buried with Christ, choosing to die with him rather than live without him, and in that moment of unity in death, God raised Jesus to life, and we too, who had been united to Christ in his death, remained united with him in his life. We have been raised with Christ through the power of the almighty God and we now live with him and will continue to do so for eternity.

How graceful is Jesus? He didn't stand back and wait until we were pure before he offered to make himself one with us, rather he became impure like we were, he was without sin, but he became sin so he could be like us in our likeness and we could be united together and be buried together in that identity. Now, by the grace of God, we have been made raised and made alive with Christ. No longer with an identity of sin, but with Christ's divine identity! Our identity is one that is holy, blameless, without blemish and righteous; for we are now children of God. It is through the grace of Christ that God has established a covenant based on his divine nature of love. Not only has he forgiven our sins freely, but he made us new in Christ with a heavenly nature and a divine relationship of sonship – just like Jesus. The cross of Christ has changed everything, for upon it everything was nailed. Jesus was nailed to the cross, so too were we, our sins and also the old covenant obligations. Jesus brought to an end all that was old: old nature, old sins, old life and old covenant, so that he could establish all that is gloriously new: new nature, new creation, new life and new covenant!

God, in his grace, has made a way for us to be in relationship with him based on the power of his love to guide us, that is Christ in us, and no longer a written code of rules and regulations. In fact, Christ died for this reality to come alive to us. He not only forgave us all our sin, but he also ensured that we would never again be enslaved by sin. He did this by establishing for us a new covenant, not a mixed covenant of old and new, but a brand new covenant of the Spirit that now leads and empowers us to live as God desires. Jesus cancelled the written code, along with its regulations, by fulfilling it through his life and then nailing it to himself in his death. He took it away so he could give us something so much better: himself! He is now living in us, and he is 'the way' that we can follow in order to live and outwork God's plans and desires in our lives.

In doing this he not only set our hearts free, but he also disarmed the powers of all spiritual enemies that are opposed to God and his children. He did this by removing any tool that could be formed against us to condemn us and make us feel unworthy to be in God's presence. For so long as there was a written obligation, that those in the spiritual realm could point to in order to expose our weakness, their was an opportunity for them to yoke us under condemnation and push us, in our minds, into separation from God – but not any longer! God has made a public spectacle of all spiritual enemies by removing their ability to condemn and invoke fear into the hearts of believers by removing his written code, that could so easily be manipulated and used to instill condemnation, replacing it with what can never be manipulated: Christ in us, our hope of glory!

Since we know this to be true, don't let anyone yoke you under condemnation because you are not fulfilling what they deem to be your 'holy oblig- ation'. Don't let people judge you by what you eat or drink, or in regards to traditional ceremonies, religious services or 'holy' days, such as the Sabb- ath. All these things that are found in the old covenant were never meant to be continued in the new covenant; rather they were a shadow of the things that were to come. The reality of all these things, however, are found in Christ.

The Sabbath, in its reality, is not a day; rather, it is the resting place we receive in Christ. For just as God finished his work of creation in six days, resting on the seventh day and inviting mankind to participate in that rest, so too did Christ finish the work of reconciliation in its fullness, so that we could finally find our rest in his finished work. The Sabbath as a shadow was a 'day', but the reality is about finding our rest in Christ. So too is it with everything in the Scriptures. They are not the reality themselves, but a shadow of the reality: that reality is always found in Christ.

So, in light of this, let's be sure we don't listen to people who try to convince us to chase after shadows, but listen to those who proclaim the reality of Christ in our lives. Don't let anyone who takes pride in false humility and who struggles endlessly to earn God's blessings by their works disqualify you from receiving God's blessings freely as a gift of his grace. Likewise, beware of those who try to gain credibility by going into great details about visions they have supposedly seen; those who are so easily overcome by their unspiritual minds that are quick to puff up all their fanciful notions.

Listen to those who are preaching Christ, his love and the power of his finished work, and not to those who have lost connection with the reality of Christ in their lives. For when someone wanders away from the reality of Christ they end up preaching about everything except Christ! Listening to such preachers won't cause you to grow in God's love and grace, because their teaching is not connected to the head from whom the whole body of Christ grows, but rather their teachings are connected merely to their own worldly ideas. Live in love together and share around the reality of Christ in your lives and in this way the body of Christ will be supported and held together in his love; growing as one body just as God desires us to grow.

Since we died with Christ to the basic principles of this world, why, as though they still have the possibility of imparting life to us, should we give any credibility to such teaching? "Do not handle! Do not taste! Do not touch!" Don't listen to these kinds of teachers. They are only capable of teaching laws, worldly principles and obligations because they don't understand the mystery of Christ in us, our hope of glory, and so they persist in preaching a message that has absolutely no power in it at all, because they are all based on human commands and teachings. Their message may indeed sound powerful with their hype and teaching techniques; and may even have the appearance of wisdom, with their focus on self-improvement, false humility and training of the flesh to perform religious obligations. The problem is that there is no power whatsoever in their message to actually empower their listeners to do the religious obligations that they have yoked upon them. If the old covenant law was powerless to help its hearers to do what it commanded, how much more can we be assured that worldly laws, philosophical ideas and 'spiritual principles' will be even more powerless to produce a transformed life? Only Christ in you can produce the transformed life that both you and God desire; and Christ in you will do it as an act of his glorious grace.

As you know, it is a living reality that we are now raised with Christ. He is no longer in the grave and neither are we; rather, we are alive and seated with him at the right hand of God. Christ has truly made himself one with us. He is here with us in our body, and we too are with him in our Spirit. Because we are already with him in the heavens, let us set our hearts on things above also. We died with Jesus in his death, and now we are alive with him in his life. Our true life is hidden with Jesus in God. Although we can already rejoice that we have been united with Christ's glorified Spirit, we also eagerly expect that when Jesus returns, he will also bless us with a glorified body like his. We will appear with him and be like him in glory.

In light of this reality, allow the Spirit that is radically alive in you to live passionately through you. Give the heavenly nature in you the permission to shine and outwork God's divine plan through you. Don't seek the things that belong to your old, earthly nature. Things that arouse lust and greed and entice you to pursue evil desires. For we know that Christ carried the punishment for all these unloving acts and passions. Remember that Jesus loved not only us, but the entire world so much that he took the wrath of God's punishment for all these unloving and self gratifying actions so that we could be free from them.

Although it's true that we all, in the past, walked in these old ways, let us remind ourselves of the far greater truth of our new life in Christ. The corrupted desires and selfish ways attached to the old life were not raised with us into our new life. They died and remained in death. So then, why would we want to wear a corpse? Why would we desire to participate in the very things that we have died to: things such as anger, rage, slander and obscene language? Rather than ignorantly indulging in the darkness of the old creation, we knowingly rejoice in the light of our new creation.

We, as children of God, are not defined by lies; rather, we are children of truth, so let us walk in our reality and speak truthfully to one another with all love and grace. The old nature has passed away, so let us also allow our old mindset to pass away with it and in its place allow the mind of Christ to outwork a life that reflects our new self, which has been made one with God. Indeed, this has already fully taken place, we are gloriously one with Jesus, so let us gladly give the Spirit permission to renew us in the knowledge of this great reality in order that we can walk as we truly are, children who have been made in the image of our Father and creator; the image of love.

In Christ we can finally see all things clearly. We see the freedom we have from all things attached to our old self, we see the freedom we have to live in the ways of God's love, and we see the freedom we have knowing we are all equal. In Christ there are no divisions. There is no ordinary or devout, no borders or nationalities, no educational divides or cultural differences, no employee or employer, but Christ is all, and he is in all.

Therefore, as God's beloved and chosen

children, holy and radically loved, wear the life you were created to wear; a life clothed with compassion, kindness, humility, gentleness and patience. Be graceful in the way you live and interact with one another, not demanding, but understanding of each others' weaknesses. If you find yourselves frustrated by one another, remember how loved you are. Remember how God does not get frustrated by your weaknesses, but rather embraces you in the midst of them and loves you all the more. Just as you have been made new like God, follow his wonderful example and let go of any grievances you may have with one another. May your life reflect God's heart and may his love, that is living and active in you, also bind together the fullness of God's nature, that abides within you, in perfect unity.

Rejoice that Christ lives in you; live with the knowledge that, despite the frustrations that people can cause you by their flaws and weaknesses, you still have a greater force of peace within you. So then, let the peace of Christ reign in your hearts, and in doing so you can witness the peace of Christ rule supreme throughout his entire body. We are so privileged to live in Christ and partake in his love, grace and divine peace. So then, let us enjoy our inheritance as equal members of Christ's body with thankful and grace-filled hearts.

Let the reality of all Christ has done for us dwell richly in you, and freely share with one another regarding this glorious reality. In doing this you will, without even realising it, encourage and teach one another in your mutual walk of faith. Let the unfailing love and grace of Jesus be upon your lips; sing, speak and live with an overflow of gratitude in your hearts to God. In whatever way you find yourselves sharing God's wonderful nature with those around you, whether it is by words or by actions, do it all knowing that Jesus is glorified in your life and it is for his name's sake you are allowing God's nature to shine. In all you do, give thanks to your beloved Father through your united life with Jesus.

Likewise, let your marriages be marked by the grace of God, not doubting or judging one another, but rather showing compassion and love towards each other. Wives, don't doubt your husbands love for you, but accept it, just as you accept Christ's love for you. Husbands, take hold of the gift God has given to you to be a living example of the love and grace of God towards your wives, not choosing to be harsh with them, but allowing the nature of God to flow through you with an abundance of love for them.

Children, though you are young, you too can live and enjoy seeing God's nature shine through you by listening and obeying your parents, for this is pleasing to your heavenly Father.

Fathers, look to the example of your heavenly

Father and be reminded daily how kind, patient and graceful he has always been to you, and let that nature be what your own children receive from you. This way they will be greatly encouraged by the love of God that shines through you so powerfully.

Employees, fulfil the duties you have been employed to do with honesty and integrity, and do so not only while your boss' eye is on you, in order to win his favour, but because you desire to live by God's nature in every situation. Whatever you do, allow your heart to be involved, and in doing so you can be assured God will also be present and active. Whatever it is you do, let the grace and power of God work through you. You are one with Christ, and everything you do is now a part of his divine life, so work knowing that what you do, however ordinary it may look to the world, is divinely significant to God. God is your very great reward, and as you allow him to shine in your workplace he will reward you also, for the truth is you are not serving man, but rather you are serving the Lord by being a light for him in your workplace. Let the love of God work through you and in turn you will also see the benefits and blessings that are born out of God's nature bear fruit.

Finally, to those who are employers, you too should allow the nature of God to shine in the way you treat your employees. Just as God is not boastful or harsh regarding his authority over you, but rather he comes alongside you with gentleness and respect, you too can follow God's good example. Be encouraging and fair to your employees, just as God is abundantly good to you.

Take advantage of your united life with Christ by sharing your thoughts and needs with him. He is always with you and you can always communicate with him, so pray freely and joyfully regarding every aspect of your lives, and pray for us too. Pray that God would open up a way for us to share his message, so that I may have the opportunity to proclaim the glorious mystery of Christ. It is for this very reason I have been placed in chains, and I'm confident that God will nonetheless make a way for me to be free once more in order that I can continue to declare the radical truth of his grace for mankind. Pray for me also, that, as God gives me opportunity to preach, I may do so in a way that clearly presents the reality of Jesus, the truth of all that he accomplished for us upon the cross and the abounding grace that is now available to all of us through him. Pray that I may present this amazing truth clearly, as indeed every preacher, including myself, should.

You too can let the truth of God's message of love shine brightly and clearly in all your interactions with those around you. Let your conversations be full of grace, for grace is God's nature, and through sharing about God from this perspective you will be able to answer everyone's questions. Grace does not judge or make accusations; on the contrary it cares and covers up weaknesses. So let God's grace be what seasons everything you say and do, and in this way his grace will be poured into the lives of those around you also.

I have sent this letter with my dear brother Tychicus and he will share with you all the news regarding my personal situation. He is a faithful preacher of God's gospel who I am thankful to work alongside as we serve God together. I asked him to deliver my letter and visit you, for I knew in advance that he would be an encouragement to you all during his stay with you, and he can also share about our current situation. I've also sent along Onesimus, who is also a faithful and grace-filled brother who can also testify to all that is happening here. I'm excited to say that there is so much going on in Rome at the moment. God is doing an incredible work. Both Luke and Mark are with me and are putting into writing an accurate account of the life of Jesus, with the express purpose of encouraging and building the Church up in the faith. I also have had incredible opportunity to share the good news to practically everyone in Rome. The brothers will give you a full report of all these good things and I'm confident that your hearts will be encouraged through hearing them.

Aristarchus, who is also in chains for the gospel, also sends his greetings, as does Mark, the cousin of Barnabas. You're aware of my instructions to you, when Mark comes to you welcome him warmly, and accept the written account of the life of Jesus that he brings to you. He wrote it with the help of Peter, who is also here in Rome, and I have also read it myself and can assure you it is in line with the truth of the gospel in every way. Justus also sends his greetings. These are my only Jewish companions among my fellow workers who are not confused about the message of God's kingdom, but understand it as it truly is: the message of God's grace. They are a blessing and a comfort to me.

Epaphras, who is one of your own, and a passionate servant of Jesus also sends his greetings. He has such a love for you all, and I can testify how much he pours out his heart in prayer to our beloved Father on your behalf. His prayer is that you would stand firm in your belief upon the good news of God's grace, and not fall victim to religion or philosophy, but rather stay grounded in the divine reality that is yours in Christ. His heart longs to see you all mature in your understanding of God's love and to walk fully assured of the unbreakable relationship of love that you now have with God through Jesus. I can testify that God is truly working powerfully in and through him, and all to your benefit, together also with those at Laodicea and Hierapolis.

My dear friend Luke, the doctor, along with Demas, send you their love. Please greet all the brothers and sisters at Laodicea and also the local believers in the surrounding towns near you. After you have read this letter, take the opportunity to share it with the other believers in Laodicea, and you in turn can also read the letter of encouragement I have recently written to them.

Please also pass on this message to Archippus: "The grace of God is at work in you, and God's empowerment is more than enough; so take heart in God's mighty strength and allow him to complete the work he has already begun in you. It is by grace you received this task, and it is by grace God will bring it to completion; only see to it that you place your confidence in the Lord through it all."

Finally, remember my chains, I'm chained for being bold enough to preach a message that no man can chain! Praise God for the freedom we have received in the gospel. Grace be with you.

PHILEMON

90

PHILEMON

Paul, chained temporarily by man, but set free eternally by Christ Jesus; together with Timothy, our mutual brother.

To Philemon my beloved friend and fellow proclaimer of God's abounding love; greetings also to Apphia our sister, Archippus our fellow freedom fighter and to all the believers who meet together in your home. Grace, love, and peace from God our Father and Jesus Christ.

My beloved brother, I must express once more how truly blessed I am by our friendship; indeed, I thank God every time I am reminded of you. It is a delight to hear of the love you have for our mutual brothers and sisters in Christ, and the encouragement you impart to them, as they continue to grow in their own faith walk, just as your own faith continues to abound in the revelation of God's love and grace. My heart is full of joy when I think of you, and I want to encourage you to continue, just as you already are, to be active in sharing your faith in the good news that God truly is graceful and abounding in love, in order that the Lord can continue to reveal the fullness of his unfailing, unending and incomparable love to your heart and mind; together with the full measure of every good thing we have been given in Christ. Enjoy the blessing of sharing the good news of God's grace. For I can testify that it is not only a joy to proclaim, but it also reminds our own hearts of all we have been given in Christ. It is so wonderful to remember you and your example of divine acceptance; you are a blessing to the whole Church, for you don't sit in judgement of others for their lack and weaknesses, but allow God's nature of love to truly shine. Your love towards those around you has blessed my heart and encouraged me greatly. Not only have you blessed my heart, but I am assured you have also refreshed the hearts of the saints you so wonderfully lift up and encourage whenever the opportunity presents itself.

In light of knowing your heart, and knowing your way of life, I rejoice that we can also relate with one another upon the basis of love. For I am assured you don't need to be convinced to do anything from a position of obligation; rather, your whole being rejoices at the opportunity to freely walk in God's nature of love. How wonderful to see the love of God so active in your life. And so, I ask of you my dear friend, bless my heart, for I am now an old man, and although this old body is also locked up by the hands of man, it is certainly not what defines me. Others may see that I am a prisoner to man, but we both know the truth, that I am a free man in the endless love of God! And, by the grace of God, that is where I will forever be kept. The worldly authorities have captured my body, but God's love has captured my heart, and in this truth I rejoice; nonetheless, your grace towards me also comforts me greatly. With this in mind, I appeal to you, on the basis of love, regarding Onesimus, who has become like a son to me during my time here in chains. Although in the past he parted company with you on bad terms, I ask that you extend grace to him now that I am sending him back to you, just as you do to everyone in your world. In the past he proved himself of little value to you, but I can assure you God has done a wonderful work in his life during his time here with me, and I am sending him back to you with the assurance that he will be a blessing, and a benefit, to you and the other believers who meet in your home.

I am sending him back to you with this letter. He has become so dear to my heart, and, truthfully, I wish I could keep him here with me in order that he could continue to help me with all the work the

Lord is doing in and through my life while I am in chains. He is a blessing to me here and is always willing to help me when I am in need, just as indeed you would be, if you were here with me. Indeed, I would be greatly blessed to keep him here with me, but in my heart I know that his place is with you, and so I send him back now. I do so knowing that we both live and trust the Spirit in us, and so I don't seek to pressure you to do anything, but rather follow the leading of the Spirit freely and trust that our God will work all things to his glory.

I don't know why Onesimus was separated from you for this period of time, but I am assured that the Lord's ways are trustworthy, and believe it is entirely possible that all this took place in order that you could now receive him back for good – no longer as merely an employee, but as a dear brother in the faith. I'm sending him back to you as proof of God's abounding grace, for he is so dear to me, and, as you will discover, even dearer to you; for God has taken what was weak and of no use, and transformed him into a man full of truth, courage and joy. He is a man you can trust, and a brother in the Lord you can embrace into God's family.

I ask that you welcome him, just as you would me, for I know how blessed my heart is every time I am in your company, and I hope that he too can also experience such a blessing. I ask that you treat his past misdeeds as God has treated ours. Forgive him my dear brother, just as I'm sure you would forgive me, and I would forgive you. Let your true nature of love be proclaimed through your grace towards him as he returns to you. If there is anything he must pay back, I will gladly take that debt upon my account. But, as we both know, we don't keep an accounts with one another, for we abide in the nature of God's grace. So then, I ask that Onesimus can come back and be embraced in the freedom and grace that is our mutual identity in Christ. I ask this not only for him, but also for myself, for it will bless my heart in such a beautiful way and I will be greatly benefited from hearing of your acceptance and love for him. Dear brother, refresh my heart in our mutual faith in Christ. I write this letter confident that you already desire to do these very things, and I already feel the joy of God's love flooding my heart as I write these words. In fact, if anything, I am sure you will do even more than I ask, for you are truly a testimony of God's abounding grace.

One more thing. Be so kind as to prepare a guest room for me, as I believe my release from this worldly prison will take place soon, and I desire greatly to visit you and rejoice once more in our friendship and time together. I know you have been praying for my release, and I am confident of God's gracious answer to your prayers on my behalf.

Epaphras, who is also here in prison with me sends his greetings. So does Mark, Aristarchus,

Demas and Luke, who are all working with me in the proclamation of God's good news to mankind.

My beloved friend, may the grace of our wonderful Lord be with your spirit.

THE GOSPEL
CANNOT BE CHAINED

Biblical Reference Text

The NIV (New International Version) is the translation I personally read, and it was the translation I used as my primary reference text for this body of work. As I stated in my foreword, this book is my own understanding and expression of what Paul originally meant in his letters. It is more of a commentary of Paul's letters that may help you see and understand his message in a fresh and positive way. Whatever Bible translation you choose to read, I hope this book has encouraged you to read the Bible more in order to search and discover the incomparable riches of Christ. I trust, and I am excited to know, that our good Lord is committed to leading you into greater revelations of his love and truth.

ACKNOWLEDGMENTS

I would like to thank my wife Mira for her consistent support; thank you for having so much grace for me during the long process of writing and completing this and other writing projects. I would also like to thank everyone who reads and interacts with me and my writing via my 'Searching for Grace' website. I'm so thankful to be able to share in your faith journey, and I want to thank you for sharing in mine. Finally, I would like to thank God, who gives me the grace to write and present his gospel message. How wonderful to belong to the the King of kings and the Lord of lords. I'm honoured to belong to the God of all grace, and thankful for the abundant grace he has poured out upon my life.

ABOUT THE AUTHOR

Mick Mooney is a passionate communicator of God's grace. He is the author of **'Look! The finished work of Jesus'** and also the creator of the popular 'Searching for Grace' comic strip (www.searchingforgrace.com). He is originally from Australia and currently resides in Germany with his wife Mira.

You can contact Mick at: mick@searchingforgrace.com

Visit Mick's website: http://searchingforgrace.com

LIGHT
VIEW
MEDIA